WHY DOES MY
CAT
Squeeze Into Boxes?

This edition published in 2018
by Susanna Geoghegan Gift Publishing
HP22 6NF, UK

Illustrations © Irisz Agocs
Contents layout: seagulls.net
Author: Michael Powell
Cover design: Milestone Creative

ISBN: 978-1-910562-66-6

Printed in China by Wai Man Book Binding (China) Ltd

CONTENTS

INTRODUCTION

CATS ARE AWESOME, BUT THEY'RE ALSO FAMOUSLY
INSCRUTABLE AND AT TIMES EVEN CAT LOVERS CAN
FIND THEM DISINTERESTED AND STANDOFFISH.

In the nine millennia since domestication, the cat-human
relationship has certainly had its ups and downs. Cats were
revered by ancient Egyptians who associated them with
their gods, but they also suffered centuries of persecution
by witch hunters.

Although cats have learned to live with humans, we
sometimes forget that they are from a different species
with unique body language, sensory equipment, social
cues and survival imperatives. In short, if you think your
cat doesn't communicate, you are greatly mistaken.

We readily believe that cats have humans completely figured out, but most of us are woefully inept at understanding their preoccupations and complex needs. We need to learn how to see into their world and recognize how their heightened senses, instinct and genetic inheritance form an important part of their psychological makeup.

Cats are more sociable than we give them credit for. For example, if your cat rubs against you and curls her tail around your legs when you come home it doesn't mean that she *wants* something. Feral cats hang around in groups and they greet each other in this way after periods of separation, so enjoy the welcome. Your cat likes you and doesn't mind showing it!

Cats are extraordinary because they agree to share our homes, on our terms, and they make the most compromises; the least we can do is to pay meticulous attention to their daily requirements. So this book answers forty-five of the most commonly asked questions about feline behaviour. Understanding how your cat communicates is a vital part of enjoying a happy and healthy friend.

Following Me To The
BATHROOM

CATS LIKE PRIVACY WHEN THEY DO THEIR
BUSINESS, WHICH IS WHY IT'S IMPORTANT TO
PUT THEIR LITTER BOX IN A QUIET PLACE RATHER
THAN A THOROUGHFARE, BUT THEY RARELY
AFFORD US THE SAME PRIVILEGE.

Some days it's impossible to visit the bathroom without a cat in tow; some owners even report closing the door only to see a cat paw poking around the threshold like a feline zombie apocalypse. Cats follow humans all over the place but what's so special about the bathroom?

There are lots of theories. If you want a humdrum explanation, your cat follows you all over the house but you probably only notice it when you want a bit of privacy, so you assume that he's only interested in you when you're on the loo or soaking in the bath.

Bathrooms often have tiled floors, which tend to be cooler than carpet, so cats seek them out when they want to cool down. The only flaw with that theory is that cats usually prefer to be warm rather than chilled out.

The prevailing speculation is that cats simply don't like being shut out. They want to be where the action is. If you shut yourself in the cupboard, your cat would be just as likely to want to join in. Fortunately that is a testable hypothesis. Experiment by shutting yourself into various parts of the house and see if your cat demands to be included!

Finally, consider that lots of interesting events take place in the bathroom with all the accompanying sounds and smells from tooth brushing, shaving and showering to the application of make-up, nostril-hair tweaking, nail clipping and of course all the toilet-related entertainment, all in a room that is acoustically very different from the rest of the house. What's not to like?

Ignoring ME

IF YOU'VE EVER SUSPECTED THAT YOUR CAT IS COCKING AN EAR IN YOUR DIRECTION WHILE FLATLY REFUSING TO RESPOND TO YOUR VOICE, YOU ARE NOT MISTAKEN – AND THERE'S EVEN A STUDY TO BACK YOU UP.

Scientists have found that cats ignore humans far more often than even we suspect and disregard their owners and strangers in equal measure.

Researchers monitored the behaviour of 20 domesticated cats in their homes for eight months and found that between 50 and 70 per cent of the cats reacted to their name by turning their heads; 30 per cent moved their ears but just 10 per cent responded – usually by meowing or moving their tails. The cats could hear their names being called but only chose to respond one in ten times.

This shouldn't be a surprise if you consider how, historically, cats started interacting with humans. Humans started farming cereal crops about 9,000 years ago. Modern cats are descended from *Felis silvestris*, a wildcat species that preyed on the rodents that were attracted to these new crops. So began a symbiotic relationship, albeit one in which cats had no requirement to obey orders (like dogs) to gain food and shelter.

The study also observes that although 'dogs are perceived by their owners as being more affectionate than cats, dog owners and cat owners do not differ significantly in their reported attachment level to their pets'. This means that domesticated cats reap all the same benefits of a having a doting owner as dogs, while conceding less cooperation. But then you knew that already, didn't you?

DRINKING
From Its Paw

CATS HAVE A REPUTATION FOR BEING FUSSY
BUT THEIR FOIBLES APPEAR TO GO INTO FELINE
OVERDRIVE WITH FOOD AND DRINK. SOME CATS
PREFER TO DIP THEIR PAW INTO A NEW BOWL
OF WATER AND THEN LICK THEIR PAW.

This seems inefficient and overly fastidious, but before you get all judgemental, this behaviour isn't so picky and it might be your fault.

New bowl

Humans have a preference for specialized drinking vessels. Most people wouldn't drink wine out of a coffee mug; many connoisseurs of the tea leaf demand the finest bone china. Cats show a similar partiality for specific types of water bowl; part of good cat care is getting this right. If your cat drinks off her paw, or from a dripping tap, it might be time to get a new bowl.

Water level

If the bowl is too narrow, the cat will have to squish her whiskers every time she takes a drink. Make sure the water level isn't too low. If your cat has to stick her head right into the bowl, this will obscure her vision, making her feel vulnerable. Plastic bowls are very common, but they are the worst for pets because they retain odours and get scratched by cleaning, allowing bacteria to thrive. Switch to ceramic or glass.

Make sure you place the water bowl in a quiet place. Your cat may resort to paw licking when drinking in a busy location, so she can stay alert to possible dangers.

Flashing Its BELLY

IF YOUR CAT IS LYING ON HIS BACK, BELLY EXPOSED AND LOOKING RELAXED, THEN THIS IS A GOOD SIGN. CATS ARE VULNERABLE WHEN THEY EXPOSE THEIR TUMMIES SO IF HE DOES IT IN YOUR PRESENCE IT MEANS HE TRUSTS YOU WON'T ATTACK HIM.

However, context is important. Just because he's looking super cute, spreadeagled and even purring, this probably isn't an invitation for you to give him a belly rub. The world doesn't revolve around you, you know. Misinterpreting his body language can actually be a clumsy breach of trust. He flashed his belly to show that he trusted you wouldn't galumph over and invade his personal space.

Cornered

A cornered cat will also resort to lying on its back so that it can make use of its claws, so paradoxically an exposed belly is also a hyper-alert defensive posture as well as a sign of relaxation. Confuse these two moods at your peril.

Risk

If you do decide to risk a belly rub, your cat will tolerate your affection, rather than enjoy it. Don't overstay your welcome or you could invite a claw or bite. If you see his claws coming out, back off. Many cats will claw or bite almost as a reflex action when their bellies are touched, or at the very least, grab your arm with their paws and start bunny kicking you. Unlike dogs, most cats don't enjoy having this area touched, so always presume that while a belly flash is the ultimate compliment, a belly rub is more for your benefit than his.

Bringing Me DEAD Animals

THERE ISN'T A CAT OWNER IN EXISTENCE WHO HASN'T HAD TO FACE THE HORROR OF A TINY CARCASS, PROUDLY DRAGGED INTO THE HOUSE BY A DOTING KITTY. SOMETIMES, THE PREY IS ALIVE, WHICH CAUSES EVEN GREATER MAYHEM, AND IT'S NOT ALWAYS SO SMALL EITHER – HEADLESS SQUIRRELS AREN'T OUT OF THE QUESTION.

So why does your cat bring you dead animals? Is it a sign that you aren't feeding her properly?

Cats have always been hunters and a mere 9,000 years of domestication isn't nearly long enough to eliminate their instinct for catching prey, even though their diet is already more than adequate. Pest control has always been an important role for cats, so humans have had no reason to selectively breed out their hunting skills. They also retain the ability to digest raw meat, so it won't harm your cat if she eats her kill.

This behaviour is most common in spayed females. Female cats bring back animals to teach their kittens how to eat (and later, when she brings live animals, how to hunt), so when she offers you a mouse or a bird she wants to pass on her expertise to you and the rest of your human family. She sees herself as your teacher and you as her pupil rather than an object of adoration.

Don't scold your cat when she brings you a dead body. If you don't like it, ignore your generous hunting guru and quietly dispose of the offending article when she's not looking.

Kneading ME

CATS KNEAD SOFT SURFACES BY PRESSING DOWN WITH ALTERNATE FRONT PAWS RHYTHMICALLY; SOME CATS ALSO INVOLVE THEIR BACK PAWS AND USE THEIR CLAWS. KNEADING IS A COMMON BEHAVIOUR IN YOUNG AND ADULT CATS BUT IT IS ONE OF THE FIRST INSTINCTIVE MOVEMENTS PERFORMED BY SUCKLING KITTENS.

Kittens knead their mother's soft tummies to stimulate the production of breast milk. Adult cats retain a happy association between soft surfaces (like cushions, and you), kneading and receiving nurture, food and comfort.

So the next time you pet your cat, if the claws come out during any kneading, he's not being aggressive; he doesn't realize that his claws are hurting, he's subconsciously reliving a happy kittenhood, so don't scold him. Adult kneading is not a reliable sign that a cat has been weaned too early.

Bonding

The kneading also serves another bonding function. Your cat has scent glands on his paws, so kneading transfers his scent onto you and marks his territory. In his own way, he's saying that you belong to him. Female cats have a further reason for kneading. They do it just before they go into heat to signal to male cats that they are ready and willing to mate.

Bedtime

Another explanation for kneading is as a bedding-down ritual, identical in function to the circling behaviour of dogs before they lie down. The kneading motion of your cat's feline ancestors would flatten grass and get rid of insects and other undesirable bedfellows.

Licking My FACE

ONE OF THE FIRST THINGS A NEWBORN KITTEN
EXPERIENCES IS THE LICK OF ITS MOTHER AS
SHE CLEANS AWAY THE FLUIDS OF BIRTH AND
STIMULATES THE BREATHING REFLEX.

The licking occurs every time the kitten returns to the nest, to imprint it with its mother's scent and to keep it clean, actions vital both for survival and for social bonding. A cat's tongue is covered with tiny backwards-facing barbs made out of keratin, so a kitty lick can feel more like a sandpaper exfoliation than a gentle display of affection.

When you receive a face lick from your cat, it is a display of affection, a transfer of scents and an act of ownership. Your cat licks to tell you that you're a trusted and complete member of her family, reinforced by her desire to clean you the way she was lovingly comforted and cleaned by her mother.

Natural

Your cat will lick any available piece of your skin, including your face, but you should try to avoid face licking, because pets have lots of bacterial organisms in their saliva. Don't reprimand her for face licking, simply distract her with another part of your body, or a toy. Licking is a natural expression of her affection so it should never be punished.

If you sense that the licking has become compulsive, either self grooming or directed towards you, it's a sign that your cat is stressed. So try to figure out any recent changes in the household or neighbourhood that could be making her anxious and distract and calm her with plenty of interactive play.

BLINKING
Slowly At Me

WHEN YOUR CAT NARROWS HIS EYES AND THEN SLOWLY BLINKS OVER SEVERAL SECONDS, HE IS SENDING YOU A 'KITTY KISS' TO LET YOU KNOW THAT HE FEELS TOTALLY RELAXED AND SAFE IN YOUR COMPANY. ALL CATS, EVEN FERAL CATS, DO THIS TO LET OTHER CATS KNOW THAT THEY AREN'T A THREAT.

Cats communicate a lot with their eyes and staring out a cat with wide eyes is considered a threat, but the slow blink says, 'See? I trust you not to attack me while my eyes are closed.'

Respect

Sometimes a slow blink can mean that your cat is open to further physical interaction, so you could slowly extend your finger to him and let him have a sniff. If he turns his head this is a neutral gesture, but if he doesn't want any further contact he will make it very clear by batting the finger away or walking away. If this happens, respect your cat's personal space and back off. However, if he sniffs your finger and then rubs his face on it, he's in the mood for a little petting.

It's fun to initiate or reciprocate a slow blink and many cats do respond to this gesture even though you're not a cat. If you wear glasses, remove them first so your cat can see your eyes. If he doesn't respond, it doesn't mean he doesn't appreciate your offer, so don't give up just because you don't get an immediate reaction. As ever when dealing with all pets, but especially cats, calm patience always yields the most satisfying results.

Putting Its TOYS In Its Water Dish

WHEN YOUR CAT DUMPS A TOY INTO HER WATER BOWL IT SEEMS LIKE A WILFUL ACT OF SABOTAGE, BECAUSE THE ACTION IS A SLOVENLY DISPLAY THAT CONTRADICTS HER OTHERWISE FASTIDIOUS NATURE, ESPECIALLY WHEN SHE DUMPS THE SOAKING WET TOY ON YOUR PILLOW. SO WHAT'S GOING ON HERE? WHY DO YOUR CAT'S TOYS GET AN EARLY BATH?

There are several factors at play here. First, the toy usually represents captured prey. Cats instinctively stash their surplus prey in a secure area of their territory. In the wild this would be a nest, but domesticated cats don't really have nesting places, so they tend to identify the feeding area – the water and food bowls – as a part of the house that belongs to them. She chooses the water bowl either

to 'drown' her prey, because she enjoys the wet texture or simply because she likes playing in the water – the bowl is as much a plaything as the wet toy and many cats enjoy this 'fishing' activity. Some cats will happily play with the water by slapping the surface to make ripples, or float objects.

Conflict

Dumping a saturated toy on your pillow is the result of the conflict between her hunting instinct and the redundancy of hunting for survival, since she is already well fed by you. She dumps it on your bed because she doesn't know what else to do with this surplus 'food' or possibly because she is entrusting you to look after it for her. Don't forget to give her a fresh bowl of water after her play session has finished.

SNEERING
When Smelling

SMELL IS A CAT'S MOST IMPORTANT SENSE. WHEN YOUR CAT WRINKLES HIS MUZZLE, OPENS HIS MOUTH IN A STATIC SNARL AND CURLS BACK HIS LIPS, HE'S NOT BEING AGGRESSIVE AND HE DOESN'T HAVE LOCKJAW! HE'S ENJOYING A SPECIALIZED TYPE OF SUPER-SMELLING CALLED THE FLEHMEN RESPONSE.

If you've never seen your cat do this, you have almost certainly seen a lion or tiger on television drawing air into their mouths while displaying this fixed snarl.

Cats have about 70 million olfactory receptor cells in their noses compared to the 5 million of humans and the area of a cat's brain dedicated to processing smells takes up more relative brain area compared to us. These two factors make a cat's sense of smell significantly more sensitive than ours and it can distinguish between thousands of odours.

Information

A cat uses scent to sniff out prey, mates and threats and to establish territory, but the Flehmen response requires a specialist 'Jacobson's organ' (aka the vomeronasal organ or VNO) – two fluid-filled sacs located in the roof of the mouth – which is mainly used to detect pheromones, chemical messengers that are secreted in sweat, excreta and other bodily fluids.

So when your cat snarls into the air it's like speed-reading the morning newspaper. He can glean masses of information about his surroundings, learn about other cats in the area and check that all is right with the world. Male cats use the Flehmen sneer more often than females even if they're neutered. This may be because they need to monitor sex-related information in their environment more frequently, such as discovering whether there are any ovulating females nearby.

Staring At
NOTHING

CATS HAVE ALWAYS BEEN ASSOCIATED WITH THE METAPHYSICAL, SO WHEN YOU SEE YOUR CAT STARING INTENTLY AT NOTHING, THE ATMOSPHERE IN THE ROOM CAN TURN A BIT EERIE. IS THERE A HUGE SPIDER BEHIND YOUR LEFT SHOULDER OR A GHOSTLY APPARITION? WHY DO YOUR CAT'S EYES LOOK SO DARK AND BOTTOMLESS? SHOULD YOU PULL YOURSELF TOGETHER OR RUN FOR THE HILLS?

Cats don't stare at nothing, silly. They always stare at something, or if not, they are listening intently or can smell something you can't, but you mistakenly assume they are being led by their vision. Even if they can see something, it doesn't follow that it's visible to the human eye.

Humans are bombarded with stimuli and our brains are very adept at filtering out most of the detail so that we can function. Cats have a much wider tolerance of sensory information, which was essential to the survival of their ancestors. In short, cats can see, hear and smell stuff that we can't, so there will always be a rational explanation for those occasions when your cat seems to be staring at thin air.

Low light

Cats are crepuscular, meaning they are active at dawn and dusk, so their eyesight is adapted for low light levels. We can see a wider spectrum of colours than cats, but they have eight times as many low light vision cells as we do. In addition to this, their range of vision is 200 degrees compared to our 180, so although we have better long distance vision, they have superior peripheral vision.

When it comes to staring, another factor to bear in mind is that cats don't need to blink as frequently as we do to keep the eyes lubricated. So they can look at something for a long time without blinking, giving the impression that they are staring with great concentration.

So if your cat appears to be staring into space, there is no need to be spooked – chances are she's simply viewing something that's invisible to you.

CHATTERING
When It Sees A Bird

FOR YEARS THERE HAVE BEEN TWO
MAINSTREAM EXPLANATIONS FOR WHY CATS
BEGIN TO CHATTER WHEN THEY ARE STARING AT
A BIRD OR RODENT THAT IS OUT OF REACH.

One reason is frustration at being stuck behind a window, or on the ground looking up at the inaccessible prey; the other is that the jaw moves in anticipation of the fatal neck bite that the cat wants to inflict on its tiny quarry. However, in the last decade a new theory has been added based on observation of the hunting techniques of wildcats.

A team of scientists were recording the vocalizations of pied tamarin monkeys in the Amazon forests when a wildcat appeared and started mimicking their calls. It was the first time that this behaviour had been documented in wildcats, and led them to speculate that all cats may hoodwink their prey using similar mimicry. The chattering behaviour in domestic cats is often triggered by the sound of a bird tweeting nearby, so the possibility that the cat is copying the bird definitely merits further study.

Some animal behaviourists believe that the chattering isn't aimed at birds but at other cats, alerting them to the presence of prey, although most cats are solitary hunters who compete for food rather than cooperate.

If you suspect that your cat is chattering out of sheer frustration, it's the perfect time to engage him in a little dangle-toy hunting play – and let him catch the toy!

Landing On Its
FEET

CATS ARE FAMED FOR THEIR ABILITY TO LAND ON THEIR FEET AFTER A FALL. THIS AMAZING SKILL IS CALLED THE 'AERIAL RIGHTING REFLEX' AND IT IS FULLY DEVELOPED BY THE TIME A KITTEN IS ABOUT SEVEN WEEKS OLD.

Cats can only do this because they have very flexible backbones, 30 vertebrae (compared to a human's 24), no collar bone and a highly developed inner ear that allows them to orientate themselves in space very precisely.

The first thing your cat will do when falling is to rotate her head so that she can spot the ground with her eyes. She pulls her front legs into her body so that the front half of her torso rotates more quickly than the back. If necessary, she will extend her back legs to slow down the rotation of her hind quarters, so that she can reach an upright falling position very quickly with all four legs beneath her.

Terminal velocity

This manoeuvre involves some complex physical laws including the conservation of angular momentum. She rotates her body around two separate axes that are tilted from one another, otherwise she wouldn't be able to stop spinning. Once her body is the right way up, she can fall like a parachute, increasing the air resistance to slow her down, helped further by her thick fur, small size and bone structure. This gives her a large body surface area in proportion to her weight, so that her terminal velocity (the maximum speed she can reach while falling) is only 60 mph (compared to 120 mph for humans).

Shock absorbers

During the final stage of descent your cat will extend her long legs and arch her back, which allows her to absorb more force when she hits the ground. Her large springy leg muscles are excellent shock absorbers, so they increase the time over which the falling (kinetic) energy is dissipated on impact, taking the force away from the bones.

Attacking My ANKLES

WHEN YOUR ANKLES BECOME THE UNWANTED
FOCUS OF YOUR CAT'S HUNTING INSTINCT, IT'S
USUALLY A SIGN THAT HE ISN'T GETTING
ENOUGH INTERACTIVE PLAY.

If he's bored he'll stalk anything that moves quickly away
from his visual field and you'll end up with bleeding ankles.
Take comfort at least that your cat doesn't hate you; he's
simply under stimulated.

Increase play opportunities throughout your house. First, set aside two or three fixed times each day when you play with him, using chasing toys so that he gets his fill of hunting small, fast-moving objects. Next, create interesting play challenges around the house for when you're away. Buy him a puzzle feeder, so he has to work his grey matter to get a food reward. If you're too lazy to get out of your chair, buy a laser light – he will spend hours chasing it while you watch television. A pole-type dangling toy is also great for safe hunting play.

Finally, make it harder for him to hide in his favourite ankle-level ambush places. Either make them inaccessible or place a motion-activated cat deterrent there. Don't punish the unwanted behaviour; this will make him anxious and more aggressive.

Instead of buying more toys, rotate them; next time he sees them they'll be interesting again. Think of ways of setting up objects to make them more interesting. For example, a ball is boring when it's on the floor, but tucked inside a cereal packet or a cardboard tube it suddenly becomes a fascinating challenge. Cats aren't that smart! They're easily entertained if you use a little imagination.

EATING
Grass

GRASS EATING IS A VERY COMMON FELINE BEHAVIOUR BUT ITS PURPOSE REMAINS UNCERTAIN, DESPITE ITS MANY BENEFITS. CATS TEND TO THROW UP AFTER EATING GRASS BECAUSE THEY LACK THE ENZYMES TO DIGEST IT, SO MOST PEOPLE ASSUME THAT CATS EAT GRASS TO HELP THEM SICK UP FUR BALLS, FEATHERS, PARASITES, MOUSE BONES AND OTHER INDIGESTIBLE FRAGMENTS THAT CAN'T PASS THROUGH THE DIGESTIVE TRACT.

There is no evidence that eating grass harms cats and it may act as a natural laxative as well as inducing vomiting. Many sources instruct cat owners to provide grass for their indoor cats. Scientists studying cats in the wild have observed that the first part of a carcass to be eaten is the intestine, which contains mainly indigestible grass fibre, although it does contain some trace minerals and the vitamins A and D. Fibre is an important component in your cat's diet, so she may munch grass if she isn't getting enough from her food.

Chlorophyll (the green pigment in grass and other plants) has many well documented health benefits in humans and animals: it purifies blood, improves the work of the liver, facilitates tissue repair and can even combat intestinal parasites and certain bacterial infections. Grass also contains folic acid, which is important for the production of haemoglobin, the iron-rich protein in the red blood cells of all vertebrates that moves oxygen in the blood.

Ultimately, it's possible that cats eat grass because they enjoy the texture and the taste. Most vets consider the behaviour normal and harmless so long as it doesn't become obsessive and the grass contains no harmful pesticides.

HEAD
Butting Me

WHILE HEAD BUTTING IN THE HUMAN WORLD LACKS A CERTAIN SOCIAL FINESSE, WHEN A CAT 'BUNTS' YOU, IT'S THE ULTIMATE SIGN OF FELINE AFFECTION, AND WHEN YOU RUB YOUR CAT'S CHEEKS AND HEAD IT HELPS THEM TO RELAX.

All cats, wild and domestic, engage in bunting to strengthen social bonds and to mark other animals as safe. Cats have scent glands on their foreheads and cheeks, so when they rub up against you or butt you in the face they deposit pheromones that label you as safe.

Every time your cat rubs against you or makes any physical contact, he leaves scent markers from glands on his paw pads, head or mouth. This is the only territory-marking behaviour that we can tolerate; the other methods are scratching and spraying urine around the place, which are definitely a lot less cute. As a general rule, the pheromones that come out of the front of your cat are affectionate and a sign of contentment, while those that come out of the rear are aggressive and communicate boundary messages like 'Keep out, this is where I live'.

Scenting

When you bring a new object into the house, big or small, from shopping bags to a new sofa, your cat will get busy scenting with its head and cheeks. You can even help him by rubbing a piece of your clothing on his head and cheeks and then rubbing the new item to cover it with your combined scent.

Sometimes when your cat is feeling frustrated, he will rub against you and other objects in a more frantic and obsessive way. This is a displacement activity to dissipate his frustration and aggression. What he really wants to do at this moment is to bite or swat you but he focuses instead on passive-aggressive rubbing. This commonly happens when he wants feeding or attention and you have been ignoring his repeated pleas.

Sticking Its
BACKSIDE
In My Face

WHEN CATS MEET FOR THE FIRST TIME THEY
OFTEN ADOPT A POSITION CALLED THE 'ELEVATOR
BUTT' IN WHICH THEY STICK THEIR BACKSIDE IN THE
AIR, TAIL HELD STRAIGHT AND BEND THEIR FRONT
PAWS SO THE HEAD IS CLOSE TO THE GROUND.
THIS IS AN INVITATION TO HAVE A GOOD SNIFF
TO SAY HELLO, MUCH LIKE DOGS DO.

Researchers have found that when one cat approaches
another cat with its tail held high, the first cat is more
likely to attract rubbing and sniffing from other members
of the cat colony. If the second cat also has its tail high,
the probability of rubbing also increases.

When your cat jumps into your lap and shows you her
backside, she is inviting you to rub alongside her. Usually
cats stand facing in opposite directions and rub along

each other's flanks to scent each other, but since we use our hands rather than our whole bodies, the cat ends up with its backside facing us.

Kittens also present their backsides to their mother as an invitation for her to groom down there. You don't have to go that far, but you can be sure that cats only present their backsides to people and animals that they really feel comfortable with, so when your cat sticks her butt in your face, she is being polite and trusting in the way she knows best.

This is a good opportunity for you to bond with her by scratching the hard to reach spot at the base of her tail. She will show her appreciation by continuing to scent you with her head, cheeks and paws; she may even start kneading you with sheer pleasure.

BURYING
Its Business

CATS BURY THEIR BUSINESS FOR TERRITORIAL AND DEFENSIVE REASONS RATHER THAN MERE CLEANLINESS. IN THE WILD THE DOMINANT CATS SUCH AS LIONS, TIGERS, LEOPARDS AND JAGUARS WILL LEAVE THEIR FAECES UNCOVERED TO LAY CLAIM TO TERRITORY.

Smaller, more submissive cats will bury theirs so they don't come into territorial conflict with the dominant animals.

Feral cats on the prowl rarely bury their faeces and often leave them in prominent positions such as a grassy tussock. However, in colonies of feral cats, a hierarchy is in operation, so the subordinates will bury and the dominant cat will often leave his faeces uncovered to advertise his dominance.

Cats will bury their faeces to escape detection from predators, especially female cats with a litter to protect. In the wild kittens instinctively dig holes for their own faeces. But if a domesticated kitten doesn't use the litter tray correctly it means he hasn't been litter trained by his mother. Healthy domesticated cats bury their business either in the litter tray or the garden because they should perceive you and any other humans in your household as dominant.

If your cat starts doing his business outside of the litter tray or doesn't bury it, it could be a sign that he believes he is dominant to you, although there could be several other explanations. Your cat could be suffering from a urinary tract infection, stomach problems or incontinence. There could be something wrong with the litter tray itself – most commonly it's either in the wrong place (it should be in a quiet, private, safe part of the house away from the eating area) or it needs cleaning (scoop out at least every other day and more frequently if you have more than one cat).

SHEDDING
So Much At The Vets

HAVE YOU NOTICED THAT WHEN YOU GO TO THE VETS, YOUR CAT SHEDS HEAPS OF FUR ALL OVER THE EXAMINING TABLE? YOU GET HOME AND FIND YOUR CLOTHES ARE COVERED TOO. SURELY CATS DON'T LITERALLY LOSE THEIR HAIR WHEN THEY'RE FRIGHTENED? OR DO THEY?

When cats are stressed or frightened they do indeed shed fur. The hairs that shed are called telogen hairs, which are no big loss because they are programmed to shed in the near future anyway; a trip to the vets merely hastens the process.

The shedding mechanism works like this: mammals have small muscles attached to the hair follicles called *arrector pili* muscles. When these muscles contract in response to fear or cold it makes the hairs stand on end, so a scared cat puffs out its tail and the fur on its back stands up all the way down the spine and the telogen hairs are released.

42

Humans have the same mechanism, only we usually experience contraction of the *arrector pili* muscles as goose bumps and we feel the hairs on our arms or on the back of our neck stand up. We too can shed large quantities of hair after a major trauma – in a telogen effluvium hair loss, hair roots are prematurely pushed into a resting phase and as much as 70 per cent of the scalp hair can fall out about eight weeks after the event.

Hair shedding at the vets is not a cause for concern. Cats shed more readily than humans, so your cat is reacting to stress, not major trauma. Shedding doesn't do the cat any harm and the hair grows back as part of the normal hair growth cycle.

GROOMING
Excessively After Being
PETTED

YOU'VE JUST HAD A RELAXING PETTING SESSION WITH YOUR BELOVED CAT AND SHE REALLY APPEARED TO BE ENJOYING IT TOO, NUZZLING INTO YOUR HANDS WITH HER HEAD AND CHEEKS, PURRING DEEPLY AND BLINKING SLOWLY.

You feel on top of the world, then your cat jumps off your lap and spends the next forty minutes painstakingly cleaning, seemingly to scrub away any trace of your existence. You feel crushed. Do you really smell that bad?

Cats are clean freaks and spend about half of their waking hours grooming. Kittens start to lick themselves after about two weeks of age and so begins a love of primping that lasts a lifetime and is a useful indicator of a cat's general level of health. An unkempt cat usually has health issues or age-related problems (such as arthritis) that make cleaning more difficult.

Cats have their own unique feline signature scent and while they conscientiously rub themselves and scratch various surfaces all over the house to spread their scent around, they don't appreciate it when you return the favour. Your hands have natural oils and pheromones, bacteria, dead skin cells and plenty more besides that interfere with a cat's smell, but also the petting rearranges the fur, which needs to be carefully licked back into place.

Cats regulate their body temperature by grooming because the saliva on the fur evaporates to cool them down, but the licking also stimulates blood flow and arranges the fur fibres for the optimum heat regulation. So when you ruffle a cat's hair-do, you're setting them up for several minutes of disentanglement. It's a good job that cats love grooming.

Moving My
SOCKS

IF YOUR CAT IS A SOCK BANDIT YOU'LL BE
WELL USED TO FISHING YOUR FOOTWEAR OUT
OF WATER BOWLS, RESCUING IT FROM THE
GARDEN AND UNDERNEATH THE SOFA OR
FINDING IT STREWN UP THE STAIRS.

Attention-seeking

So long as your sanity can handle this petty thievery, there's no harm in it (unless your cat starts eating your socks), although it could be a sign that he's anxious or bored and wants to play.

The most likely explanation is that your cat has learned that when he steals something he usually gets your attention. Even if he gets a good scolding, it's better than being ignored. Better still, if you end up chasing him throughout the house, he gets a big payoff. Don't scold or punish – just play more with your cat. Some owners report that their cats have a special vocalization reserved for sock shifting, usually a loud and excessive mewing. This is most likely part of the attention-seeking routine, although it can often feel more existential.

Nesting

Some experts suggest that female cats may be displaying nesting instincts, picking up socks and moving them around like kittens, but the lure is probably much wider than this – your cat is attracted to the texture, the smell and the appearance of the stolen items and wants to play with them. But first he must move them away from your sight, because he knows that you'll take them off him.

Many owners report sock and clothes stealing as a primarily nocturnal pursuit. Once again, a separation anxiety/attention-seeking explanation fits well here, because it takes place when everyone else in the house is asleep.

Squeezing Into Little BOXES

EVERYONE KNOWS THAT CATS LIKE TO SQUASH THEMSELVES INTO IMPOSSIBLY SMALL SPACES. A TINY BOX OR EVEN A PLASTIC BAG BECOMES PRIME REAL ESTATE IN A CAT'S MIND, BUT IT'S A LITTLE HARDER TO UNDERSTAND WHY THEY MAKE THIS CHOICE, BEYOND THE OBVIOUS, 'BECAUSE THEY CAN'.

Animals that prey on cats, such as coyotes, birds of prey and raccoons, are generally bigger and less flexible than their prey, so a cat can easily put itself out of reach by squeezing into a small space. But she can just as easily scamper up a tree, so she does have other options. Clearly feeling secure is a major motivator. Cats prefer to run away and hide from conflict rather than fight and they respond to environmental and psychological threats by decreasing their activity.

A small hiding place also makes your cat invisible to her own prey and reduces the amount of her body odour than can reach the air to alert a mouse or bird to her presence. In your home, you'll find that you're usually the prey, which is why you get ambushed by a paw under the bed as you walk past, or the cat jumps you from a confined hiding place.

Cosy

Cats enjoy basking in the sun, but they also curl up when they want to preserve body heat, so squeezing into a tight space can also help to regulate body temperature. Small places are simply cosier. Humans seek similar solace – curling up on the sofa under a duvet while watching television is more comforting and relaxing than merely sitting.

SITTING
On My Keyboard

ANY CAT OWNER KNOWS THAT CATS FIND
COMPUTER KEYBOARDS IRRESISTIBLE AND IF YOU
HAD TO GUESS WHY, YOU'D PROBABLY SAY THAT
THEY LIKE THE HEAT GENERATED BY YOUR LAPTOP
AND ARE ALSO TRYING TO GET YOUR ATTENTION.

You'd be right, but that's not the whole story. Your keyboard provides a multi-sensory experience for your cat with the added bonus of human attention.

The keyboard of a laptop gives off heat, but it also has lots of moving parts that make a clicking sound and move up and down. Your hands are also moving rapidly which is fascinating for cats. When your cat steps onto the keys, they move underneath his paws; when he lies down and shifts his weight, they ripple beneath his belly. Then there's the screen – bright blinking lights and objects moving quickly, once again accompanied by sounds. It's not just a computer – it's a feline activity centre.

Pawing

So when your cat lies down on your keyboard he knows he can either go to sleep, or he will get petted by you, or he'll have a front-row seat to catch all the fascinating activity happening on your screen – much better than chasing a laser pointer. The cursor looks like a bug, so naturally that requires some investigation too and plenty of screen pawing.

Discourage

If you want to discourage your cat from monopolizing your computer so you can actually get some work done, try setting up a comfy cushion or blanket next to your keyboard so he can still enjoy your company. Don't encourage him by showing him things on your screen (like your new swimming goldfish screensaver) and put the keyboard out of reach when you're not using it, so he doesn't take it over in your absence.

PAWING
The Ground By The Food Bowl

PAWING IN OR AROUND THE BOWL AFTER EATING IS ANOTHER ONE OF THOSE REDUNDANT INSTINCTS THAT STILL LINGER IN YOUR CAT. IT'S A CALL BACK TO WHEN WILDCATS COVERED UP WHERE THEY'D BEEN TO PROTECT THEMSELVES FROM PREDATORS AND ALSO TO KEEP A LOW PROFILE WITH ANY PREY ANIMALS IN THE AREA.

She's not saving food for later; she's trying to hide the bowl and any leftovers. If she had a power hose or a camouflage net she'd use them. In fact, some cats do go as far as dragging a rug or towel over their empty bowl.

If the pawing becomes obsessive or she starts dragging your guest towels into her eating area, the best solution is to take away the problem. Put the dish in the sink to soak, or better still, wash it, dry it and put it away in a cupboard until the next meal time. If she still scratches, distract her with another activity.

Fussing

If your cat isn't a post-prandial floor scratcher but suddenly starts fussing and pawing the ground around her bowl it may be because she doesn't like the food, especially if you've recently changed it. If you do have to change her food you should introduce it gradually over a seven-day period to avoid upsetting her digestive system and also because the change will unsettle her.

Otherwise, this instinctive behaviour is natural and harmless, so if it doesn't bother you and the cat walks away contentedly afterwards, there's no cause for concern.

Imitating A
BABY

STUDIES HAVE SHOWN THAT A CAT'S CRY FOR FOOD OR ATTENTION SHARES MANY ACOUSTIC CHARACTERISTICS WITH A CRYING HUMAN BABY. HUMAN ADULTS ARE BIOLOGICALLY PROGRAMMED TO RESPOND TO THIS SOUND, WHICH CREATES A HEIGHTENED SENSE OF AGITATION AND DISCOMFORT.

Thousands of years of interaction between cats and humans have made this convergence almost inevitable. In fact, scientists have discovered that cat meows are more generic than most cat owners would believe. Meows are strident because they need to attract attention, but beyond this, cats communicate with their owners with much less subtlety than we give them credit for.

In a recent study published in the *Journal of Comparative Psychology*, researchers from the Cornell University

Department of Psychology asked cat owners to interpret meows taken from 12 cats in five behavioural contexts. Their accuracy was slightly greater than chance, but not enough to be significant. The researchers concluded that 'meows are nonspecific, somewhat negatively toned stimuli that attract attention from humans'. It seems likely that in so far as meows display any subtlety, real or imagined, humans are surprisingly poor at interpreting it.

Most cat owners would argue against this. They are convinced that their cat has distinct cries for different situations: one meow for 'I want attention', another for 'I'm hungry' and another still for 'I'm angry', but the cat has simply learned to use whichever vocalizations provoke a human response; or rather, humans have conditioned themselves to respond to certain sounds by attaching meaning to them and neglecting other sounds by offering no anthropomorphic interpretation.

The familiar saying, 'Dogs have masters, cats have servants' should be amended to 'willing servants whose servitude is perpetuated by their stubborn insistence that meows have a repertoire of subtle meanings'.

Sucking And Chewing My
SWEATER

WOOL SUCKING IS MOST PREVALENT IN CATS UNDER ONE YEAR OF AGE. SOME CATS CONTINUE THIS BEHAVIOUR INTO ADULTHOOD, USUALLY BECAUSE THEY HAVE BEEN WEANED TOO EARLY.

Sucking on blankets, sweaters, cushions, carpets or shoe-laces can be a sign that the cat has been removed from its mother prior to the recommended twelve weeks. Suckling provides comfort and the soft warmth of the wool offers a similar tactile experience to the mother's belly.

If your adult cat persists in wool sucking behaviour, you should mention this to your vet, because there are health implications. If she accidentally swallows lots of fibres or if the behaviour escalates into pica (persistent and deliberate ingestion of non-nutritious materials), she could develop intestinal problems. She may also be lacking something in her diet (such as dietary fibre, although this is rare) or have an underlying medical condition such as anaemia or diabetes. There is also a genetic component, since wool sucking is most prevalent in Oriental breeds (which tend to have a longer nursing period).

Sometimes cats revert to wool sucking at times of stress, such as the arrival of a new baby or pet, a house move, death, divorce, or a change in your daily routine. Alternatively it might be a sign of boredom. The best way to discourage wool sucking is to distract your cat with interactive play when she starts to suck, and remove the garment or object so she can't return to suckling afterwards.

Every cat should have a predictable schedule of daily interactive play to stay mentally and physically stimulated. Also, enrich her environment during the day (especially when you are away), by providing puzzle feeders or a cat tree, and rotate several stimulating solo toys.

SLEEPING
So Much

MANY CAT OWNERS WORRY THAT THEIR CAT SLEEPS TOO MUCH AND FEEL GUILTY THAT THEY AREN'T PROVIDING ENOUGH STIMULATION. THEY CAN RELAX BECAUSE CATS ARE ONE OF THE BIGGEST SLEEPERS OF THE ANIMAL KINGDOM, TYPICALLY DOZING BETWEEN 16 AND 20 HOURS A DAY (YOUNG AND OLD CATS SLEEP THE LONGEST), BUT IT ISN'T BECAUSE THEY'RE LAZY.

Thousands of years of evolution have selected characteristics for feline predators that conserve every calorie so they can use quick bursts of energy-draining speed to catch their next meal. Even when a kill is achieved, being able to save energy between kills makes the difference between life and death.

Cats have a high protein diet, so they don't need to spend hours grazing like herbivores. Once they've eaten their prey, they can have a nap: they sleep because they can and they must. Your cat doesn't have to catch his prey; his food bowl magically fills up each day, but his instinct still tells him to sprawl out on your bed for hours on end to get plenty of shut-eye.

Most of this sleep takes place during the day because most cats (apart from cheetahs) hunt during the early morning or evening (and especially the moonless part of the night), when it is cooler and easier for them to approach their prey with stealth, aided by their low light vision.

Many cat owners also believe that their cats are awake all night, but this isn't true. If your cat continually disturbs your sleep with its nocturnal activities, provide more interactive toy play during the day to keep him awake. Also install a window perch (with a good view of your bird table) so he's motivated to stay alert and study what's happening outside.

GOING CRAZY
And Tearing Around The
HOUSE

CATS ARE FAMOUSLY INSCRUTABLE BUT NOTHING QUITE PREPARES YOU FOR YOUR CAT'S FUNNY FIFTEEN MINUTES. WITHOUT WARNING, SHE STARTS ZOOMING AROUND THE HOUSE FOR NO APPARENT REASON. DOES SHE KNOW SOMETHING YOU DON'T? OR IS SHE TRYING TO COMMUNICATE WITH YOU? HERE ARE A FEW REASONS WHY YOUR CAT IS ACTING CRAZY.

The most likely explanation is that she spends most of her life sleeping and occasionally needs an outlet for her bottled-up energy. When she's feeling amped up, a noise or a smell can be enough to trigger an episode of feline flapdoodle. She may have spotted an intruder through the window, invading her precious territory, or heard another cat staking a claim. If she scampers from window to window you can be fairly sure that something outside the house has set her off.

It's also a possibility that she's chasing prey. Just because you can't see or hear the mouse in the next room doesn't mean your cat can't. So it's action stations. All that sleeping prepares her for these precise moments of high alert. If she brings you a gift ten minutes later, you have your answer.

Restless

Check her fur for flea dust, especially around her neck. All that scratching can drive any animal insane, so if your cat does more tearing around the house than usual and is restless and irritable or grooms obsessively, you may have been neglecting her flea treatment. Don't delay because a flea infestation can cause anaemia on top of the itching misery.

Daily kitty crazies are completely normal but if they happen several times a day, often accompanied by rippling or rolling of the skin on her back, take her to the vet to test for a rare brain affliction called Hyperesthesia syndrome. Otherwise, sit back and enjoy the show.

LICKING
Plastic Bags

LOTS OF OWNERS REPORT THAT THEIR CATS ENJOY LICKING PLASTIC BAGS. SOME HAVE A PREFERENCE FOR REFUSE BAGS, OTHERS FOR SHOPPING BAGS. IT'S A CURIOUS HABIT THAT DEFINITELY WARRANTS FURTHER INVESTIGATION.

If your cat is a bag licker, you can be certain that he derives one or several sensory rewards from the activity. So let's consider what those might be.

The plastic has a smooth texture, which your cat may find satisfying; it also makes a noise so it provides aural stimulation. You bring the bags into the house from outside along with lots of environmental smells and tastes, including traces of food that were inside them. Some biodegradable bags contain cornstarch, which may give the bags an interesting flavour.

There are two main types of non-degradable plastic shopping bag. The lightweight single-use bags are made from high density polyethylene or HDPE, while the heavier 'bags for life' are made from low density polyethylene or LDPE. Both are very safe and inert and are not known to leach any harmful chemicals, so your cat isn't doing himself any harm. Any taste from the bag itself is most likely from the inks used to print store logos and other designs.

Be vigilant

Some sources claim that plastic bags mimic a pheromone found in male cat urine but this myth has probably arisen because of another food packaging plastic called polyethylene terephthalate or PET, which degrades with time and leaches chemicals called phthalates which disrupt the body's hormones, but this isn't used for plastic bags.

So if your cat likes licking plastic bags, let him have his fun but remain vigilant and remove them if he tears and chews them up and starts swallowing.

Sitting On The Person Who
HATES CATS

IT'S WELL KNOWN THAT WHEN A CAT WALKS INTO A ROOM FULL OF PEOPLE IT WILL MAKE A BEELINE FOR THE ONE PERSON WHO FEELS VERY UNCOMFORTABLE AROUND CATS. HOW DOES SHE KNOW – AND IS SHE BEING SPITEFUL OR JUST TRYING TO BREAK DOWN BARRIERS?

Well, of course the cat doesn't have any of the motives, devious or otherwise, that we might want to impose on her. The real reason is because of the body language of the cat-shy person compared to everyone else. A cat dislikes direct eye contact and sees it as a threat, so when she slinks into a room and everyone stares at her, cooing and sticking out their arms for a stroke, she doesn't want anything to do with them. Instead she'll seek out the person who is sitting quietly, looking away – the least threatening human in the throng, the one who is respecting her boundaries and maybe throwing her the odd glance, then turning away. Cats find that irresistible.

The closer she approaches the cat-shy individual, the stiffer they become. They may even close their eyes briefly as they cringe inwardly. The cat interprets this as a slow blink – the signal of being trusting and open to further physical interaction. She comes closer and the cat-shy person slowly extends an arm to fend off the approaching feline, but the cat interprets this as a polite invitation to get better acquainted. Finally, if the cat hater unwillingly strokes the cat, it will be brief, leaving the cat wanting more, so she jumps onto a nice warm lap and waits to be petted.

CRYING
In The Middle Of The
NIGHT

CAT OWNERS COMMONLY COMPLAIN THAT
THEIR CATS CRY LOUDLY AND SOMETIMES
INCESSANTLY THROUGHOUT THE NIGHT.

This behaviour is especially common in older cats, but it can quickly become a habit at any age if the cat learns that it can get your attention and even get you to do its bidding (e.g. feeding at 5am) during the night. So, cats cry during the night for a reason, but it is important that you understand the cause rather than merely try to pause the cacophony.

Kittens meow to their mothers to tell them that they're hungry, cold, scared or lonely. When they get older they use a repertoire of about a hundred vocalizations to communicate with other cats that includes hissing, growling, trilling and chattering. But adult cats rarely meow at each other. They reserve this infantile form of communication for us, because we are pitifully inept at understanding their more nuanced sounds and usually misinterpret their subtle body language as well.

Reassurance

The main reason cats meow at night is because they want attention or reassurance, or because they are bored. If your cat suddenly starts night-time meowing, try to figure out if there have been any changes in his routine, such as a member of the household leaving, having new carpet installed, changes to your work patterns, etc.

You can reduce anxiety by making sure he has plenty of retreats where he can feel safe as well as increasing interactive play and stimulation during the day and minimizing environmental changes where possible (e.g. turning down loud music). You can relieve boredom by hiding a few snacks around the house, and making sure he has toys to play with when he wakes up (even a new cardboard box can break the habit for one night).

Pestering Me While I'm On The
PHONE

CATS CAN BE AT THEIR MOST ANNOYING WHEN WE'RE ON THE PHONE; THE MORE IMPORTANT THE CALL, THE BIGGER NUISANCE THEY SEEM TO MAKE OF THEMSELVES. SO WHAT IS IT ABOUT TALKING INTO A SMALL PLASTIC BOX THAT MAKES THEM SO NEEDY?

Doesn't your cat know you are talking on the phone? No. She doesn't. She probably thinks you're talking to her. You could be holding a banana up to your ear for all she cares. All she hears is the stream of noises coming out of your mouth, accompanied by non-threatening body language (i.e. you're not staring at her), so she figures it's a good time to approach.

The other attraction is the predictability of your routine. When the phone rings, your cat knows that you will pick it up and then sit on the sofa or stairs, or stand in the hall – cats like predictability. She also knows that you'll be stationary for a few minutes, which is the perfect opportunity for some petting.

In fact, phone calls are the perfect opportunity for you to increase your cat's sense of security and wellbeing, by giving her some fuss every time you are on the phone. Enjoy her desire to be close to you. She's not doing you any harm and if the inevitability of her needy behaviour irritates you, flip that feeling around and be mindful that you can give her just what she craves – security and predictability.

SPRAYING

CATS SPRAY TO MARK THEIR TERRITORY AND
THIS BEHAVIOUR IS MOST COMMON AMONG
UNNEUTERED MALES. IF YOUR CAT STARTS
SPRAYING AROUND THE HOUSE, NOT ONLY IS
IT UNPLEASANT AND UNHYGIENIC FOR YOU,
IT'S A SIGN THAT HE IS STRESSED AND ANXIOUS.

First of all, establish that your cat is spraying and not simply urinating. Cats spray by depositing a small amount of urine on a vertical surface; they urinate by squatting to eliminate a larger volume of urine on a horizontal surface. If your cat is urinating, he may have a bladder infection, or you might need to clean or move the litter tray or provide an additional one. If he is spraying, you should first of all ask your vet to check him over for any underlying health issues. If you can rule out a physical cause, then you need to either eliminate or compensate for the conflict inside or outside the house that is causing the stress.

For tomcats, neutering is an effective way to reduce the sex hormones that cause the spraying behaviour:

nearly 80 per cent of male cats stop spraying after being castrated.

Causes

A common cause is a new dog or cat coming into your cat's territory or a new pet within the home. Talk to your vet about temporary separation, desensitization and counter-conditioning strategies. If the issue is outside, temporarily limit his view of the garden so he can't see the intruder; if he's an outdoor cat, keep him indoors for a few days to restrict his contact with the source of his anxiety. Unfortunately, overcrowding in a multi-pet home often results in excessive spraying.

Treat spray areas with an enzyme cleaner and then either feed or play with your cat in that area to build up positive associations to replace the anxiety. It's important to break the habit in this way, otherwise your cat will feel the need to return to the scene of the crime to top up a fading scent.

You can also reduce anxiety by giving your cat plenty of attention and increasing interactive play, using a variety of toys on rotation.

Scratching The
FURNITURE

CATS SCRATCH TO SHARPEN THEIR CLAWS
(BY REMOVING THE OUTER HUSKS) AND TO
REMAIN LIMBER. THEY CHOOSE A SURFACE
THAT OFFERS RESISTANCE BECAUSE THEY
NEED TO EXERCISE THE FORELIMBS.

They also need to stretch the spine, so the height of the scratching object is equally crucial. If your cat is using the furniture to perform this important claw and body maintenance, it could be either a territorial issue or mean that the scratching post you provided is either unsuitable or in the wrong place. If the scratching is widespread throughout the house, your cat is displaying insecurity.

Cats frequently scratch outdoors, often on tree bark, but if there are lots of cats in your area, your cat may prefer to do most of her scratching within her secure home environment, so it's vital that you supply a suitable scratching post, one for each cat you own. It needs to be high enough to allow her to scratch at full stretch and it needs to be placed somewhere that she actually likes to be. Cats often scratch after sleeping, so placing a post next to a favourite sleeping spot is also helpful.

Scratching releases scent from sweat glands in between the pads of the feet, so once a piece of furniture, wall or carpet has become a scratching place you need to remove the scent with an enzyme-based cleaner. Wooden surfaces can also be sanded and treated with furniture polish to make them smooth and uninviting.

Drooling When
HAPPY

MANY CAT OWNERS REPORT THAT THEIR
CATS DROOL WHEN THEY ARE HAPPY; THEY
ONLY OBSERVE THIS BEHAVIOUR WHEN THEIR
CAT IS BLISSED OUT, OFTEN ACCOMPANIED BY
PURRING WHILE BEING BRUSHED OR PETTED.

Sometimes the drool is slight and other times it can be torrential from the same cat. Some cats never drool. So what's the deal with your salivating kitty?

Vet check

Firstly, if your cat suddenly develops a new drooling habit, check with your vet that he isn't suffering from mouth ulcers, tooth damage, tartar build-up, gum disease or poisoning. Once these have been ruled out, congratulations – you have a very happy cat and there's no cause for alarm.

Theories

There is a theory that happy droolers are so relaxed that they forget to swallow. Try gently touching your feline's nose with your fingertip to trigger the swallowing response. If the drooling is accompanied by kneading, the salivating can be easily explained: your cat is recreating the kneading action he used as a kitten to stimulate his mother's breast milk. Even though there's no milk on offer today, it doesn't stop his saliva glands from going into overdrive.

Some owners note that their cats only drool while they are purring and speculate that some cats are unable to do both simultaneously. All cats are wired differently so this is certainly a plausible explanation. Alternatively it may just be that when certain areas of the body are stimulated by petting, such as the back, neck, cheeks and chin, it triggers the cat to start salivating. It's also possible that some cats relax their facial muscles so much that they turn into a sprinkler system.

Currently there is no definitive answer, so this behaviour needs further study. If you have a happy drooler, experiment at home to spot the triggers.

Needing An
ESCORT
To Its Food Bowl

YOUR CAT'S FOOD BOWL IS IN THE PRECISE SAME PLACE IT WAS YESTERDAY AND EVERY DAY BEFORE, RIGHT BACK TO WHEN IT WAS A KITTEN.

But for some reason every day she mews plaintively and insists that you remind her of its whereabouts. Some hungry cats even yowl at night until their weary owners get out of bed to guide them to a bowl that is brimming with food. Sound familiar? Does your cat have no short-term memory or is she unbelievably stupid?

Pattern

Actually it's easy for this kind of behaviour to become a pattern. Your cat will always make a connection between you and her food because you always provide it; you are the means by which it always ends up in her bowl. So that association becomes hard wired within the first few weeks of your weaned cat's life.

Some cats like company while they eat, so they don't need reminding where their bowl is, but they enjoy leading you there so that they can eat with you nearby. Your cat gets the reward of food plus your attention. During the night the 'game' is even more gratifying because that's the time when she habitually gets ignored by sleeping humans. Once you give in a few times and escort her to her bowl, you will be doomed to repeat the ritual until you can set up an alternative scenario.

Notice that your cat has no trouble finding her bowl when you are out; she mysteriously only needs help when you're at home – further proof that your acquiescence has contributed to this power play ritual. Unless your cat is old, infirm or vision impaired, you can break the habit by leaving her filled bowl and walking away. Hunger will soon trump stubbornness.

WAVING
Its Tail From Side To Side

CONTEXT IS OFTEN IMPORTANT WHEN INTERPRETING FELINE BODY LANGUAGE, BUT NEVER MORE SO THAN WHEN A CAT WAGS ITS TAIL. THIS GESTURE HAS MULTIPLE MEANINGS AND YOU HAVE TO USE A BIT OF DEDUCTION TO FIGURE IT OUT. MISINTERPRET THE TAIL WAG AT YOUR PERIL.

A relaxed cat swishes its tail lightly and casually from side to side when it is feeling thoughtful or indecisive, sizing up a situation. If only the tip is twitching, he is feeling unsure and nervous. He might be planning to jump up to a high surface but he can't be sure that he's going to make it. In this context the tail swish shows that he's feeling uncertain and is mustering up the courage.

A very relaxed cat, curled up with eyes closed, apparently fast asleep, may give a tail swish when you call his name, just to acknowledge you when he's feeling too lazy to open his eyes.

The tail swishes quickly and erratically when a cat is feeling curious or playful, or is hunting. When a cat can't see its stationary prey it will twitch its tail to make the prey react, so it's often the precursor to the cat's pounce. He will display this same behaviour when playing with other cats, and mother cats teach their kittens to hunt using this tail twitch. When your cat watches a bird through the window he'll often twitch his tail to indicate that he's eager to hunt.

Finally, when your cat waves his tail quickly and violently from side to side in a wide arc, it's time to back off. This gesture means he's feeling intense distress, fear, annoyance or aggression. He is preparing to flee or attack. If he does this while you are petting him, he wants you to stop, otherwise his annoyance will escalate to a paw swipe or a bite.

Reacting To
CATNIP

IF YOUR CAT IS SUSCEPTIBLE TO CATNIP SHE WILL
SHOW HER APPRECIATION WITH ONE OR MORE OF
THESE BEHAVIOURS: ROLLING IN IT, RUBBING HER
FACE IN IT, DROOLING, CHASING AROUND THE
ROOM AND EVENTUALLY ZONING OUT.

After about ten minutes her 'high' will end and she won't
respond to catnip again for at least 30 minutes. About 75
per cent of cats react to catnip because it is an inherited
trait. Kittens, however, don't react to catnip until at least
six months of age.

Catnip (*Nepeta cataria*) is a perennial herb and member of the mint family. It is highly aromatic and smelling it appears to generate the most extreme reaction in cats. The active ingredient, a volatile oil called nepetalactone, enters the cat's nose and binds to protein receptors that stimulate sensory brain cells, most notably the olfactory bulb which is located at the front of the cat's brain. This sends messages to the hypothalamus which tells the pituitary gland to release feel-good chemicals. The cat essentially has a sexual response to the catnip, similar to exposure to cat pheromones, which is why the physical reaction shares much in common with cats in heat.

Eating catnip has a sedative effect. Despite the apparent drug-like response, catnip isn't addictive or harmful, although excessive exposure can cause vomiting and diarrhoea. Frequent exposure also decreases sensitivity, so it is recommended you only bring out the catnip once every two or three weeks.

Another curious property of catnip is that it is ten times more effective at repelling mosquitoes than DEET, although it is less effective on human skin than on clothing. It also repels cockroaches, flies and termites.

Smelling My
BREATH

IF YOUR CAT SMELLS YOUR BREATH HE'S NORMAL, WELL ADJUSTED AND CURIOUS. CATS LIKE TO GLEAN AS MUCH INFORMATION AS THEY CAN ABOUT THEIR SURROUNDINGS AS WELL AS THE PEOPLE WHO MATTER IN THEIR LIVES (WHO WOULD FEED HIM IF ANYTHING HAPPENED TO YOU?).

Familiar cats greet each other in a similar way, sniffing each other's noses and mouths, which might lead on to head rubbing and mutual grooming.

Cats can tell a lot about your physical and emotional health by smelling you, and your breath reveals what you've eaten, the state of your digestive tract and your gum and tooth health, which are all indicators of whether or not you'll be around next week to operate a tin opener. They can also tell whether you've interacted with other cats or humans.

Reciprocate

Early morning bed breath seems to hold a special attraction, but that's probably because it's the first opportunity for several hours and is part of a more general rise and shine greeting routine. Many cat owners report that breath smelling often occurs after they have eaten. Naturally, your cat is curious to know what you have eaten because food plays a very important role in his life and so checking out your eating habits feeds into his culinary preoccupations – food is a primal drive for all animals but especially carnivorous predators like cats.

While your cat is sniffing your breath, return the compliment to check out his own health. If it makes you wince, your cat may have a health problem. By far the most common cause is gum disease caused by a build-up of plaque. Visit your vet for a scrape and polish, because inflamed gums are always painful and can be life threatening. Another common cause is that he has something stuck between his teeth or underneath the gums. To prevent most kitty bad breath, brush your cat's teeth every day using special feline toothpaste.

HISSING

CATS HISS WHEN THEY ARE SCARED AND FEEL THREATENED, BUT IT DOESN'T MEAN THEY ARE ABOUT TO ATTACK. IN THE WILD A SINGLE CAT BITE CAN EASILY BECOME INFECTED AND LEAD TO DEATH, SO A CAT WANTS TO AVOID FIGHTING AT ALL COSTS.

The hiss is a warning designed to make the threat go away so that fighting is unnecessary.

Cats hiss by forcing air through an arched tongue. Your cat will also pull her lips back and flatten her ears against her head (this protects them if the situation escalates into a fight). Many behaviour experts say that a cat's hiss mimics the frightening hiss of a snake, since snakes are one of the most deadly and feared animals.

It is always in a cat's best interests not to fight, so if you are confronted by a hissing cat you still have time to avoid attack by removing yourself. If the threat persists, the cat will have no option but to resort to violence. Don't approach or reprimand a hissing cat; move slowly away, avoiding eye contact. Once a cat is hissing you can't placate it by extending your hand so it can sniff you and recognize that you aren't a threat. You have already passed the point of negotiation, so if you are foolish enough to continue whatever behaviour is causing the cat to hiss, you can expect to get scratched or bitten.

It's natural for cat owners to feel affronted when their cat hisses at them and want to reprimand or reassert their dominance. Remember that your cat is hissing because she feels threatened, so try to figure out what is causing her fear rather than punishing her for expressing it. Walking away from a hissing cat isn't a sign of weakness. Ignoring unwanted behaviour is acceptable so long as you also make the effort to reward desirable behaviour. Your cat will learn that being calm and friendly yields positive results.

BEGGING
For Food

CATS ALWAYS SEEM TO BE BEGGING FOR FOOD.
MANY CAT OWNERS REPORT BEING PLAGUED
INCESSANTLY BY THEIR CATS, JUMPING UP ON THE
TABLE WHEN THEY'RE EATING, FOLLOWING THEM
AROUND LOOKING EMACIATED AND STANDING
NEXT TO THEIR EMPTY FOOD BOWLS WAILING.

Many give their cats plenty of human scraps on top of a generous supply of cat food, so why does the cat appear to be so obsessed with food?

If your cat stands at an empty bowl whining, there's a good chance it's food related, but have you ever considered that you may be misinterpreting all the other times the cat approaches you? It likely that your cat just wants your company. It's so easy to perpetuate the greedy cat narrative if you make the assumption that every time they come near you they are demanding to be fed. If you then feed them, their attention-seeking behaviour is always rewarded with food and the simple demand for company is neglected.

If you are genuinely concerned that your cat is obsessed with food and permanently hungry, take him to the vet to check for worms, hyperthyroidism or diabetes and to reassure you that his cat food is meeting his nutritional needs. Once any problems have been ruled out, the other most likely causes of genuine food obsession are depression and loneliness, both of which can be helped by giving your cat more attention and affection.

Food is a biological imperative, so your cat's eyes widen and he will get excited when food is offered, but he will also react the same way to stimulation, focused play and human interaction. It's lazy and cruel for you to respond to every call for attention by checking to see if the food bowl is empty.

PACING
Around The House Moaning

IF YOUR UNSPAYED FEMALE CAT WALKS AROUND THE HOUSE MOANING AND YOWLING INCESSANTLY, IT MEANS THAT SHE'S IN HEAT (ESTRUS) AND SEARCHING FOR A MATE.

She can stay in heat for seven to ten days and she can come into heat several times a year, so along with her attention-seeking behaviour and anxiety, you have a very challenging week and a half ahead of you.

When a cat is in heat her scent changes, so naturally she is eager to spread this around as much as possible to advertise to potential suitors. Don't be surprised if she rubs against your legs so frequently that you nearly trip over her. She will rub against you and objects much more than usual and commando crawl while sticking her backside in the air and/or roll around on the floor wailing. If you rub her lower back you will see the 'tail deflection reflex' – she will stick her backside in the air and move her tail to one side.

Keep her indoors and secure doors, windows and cat flaps so she can't escape and male cats can't break into the house. Drawing curtains will also obstruct her view of the outside world and calm her down, but you might feel this is a step too far.

Give your cat lots of affection and fuss during this difficult time. She may be annoying now, but if you don't try to calm her down she'll drive you bonkers. Your gentle physical contact should help to soothe her and make her feel less restless. Also step up the interactive play, which will help take her mind off her relentless urge to find a mate. Ultimately, the best solution is to have your cat spayed, which will prevent further instances of this behaviour, not to mention a litter of unwanted kittens.

Climbing
TREES

FERAL AND OUTDOOR CATS LIKE TO CLIMB TO HIGH PLACES BECAUSE SOMETIMES THE THRILL OF THE HUNT LEADS THEM THERE, WHILE OTHER TIMES THEY ARE TRYING TO AVOID RIVAL CATS OR PREDATORS.

Also, cats like to get a good view of their neighbourhood and the best way to get the lowdown on the area is to get as high up as possible. A vantage point not only keeps a cat away from predators; it also helps them to see potential dangers and prey.

Climbing is excellent exercise for your cat and they are well suited to it with their flexibility and strong muscular legs and backs. They evolved from the tree-dwelling weasel-like carnivorous genus Miacis in the Late Palaeocene (55 million years ago) which are the common ancestors of both cats and dogs. However, their bodies are best designed for climbing upwards, which is why they sometimes get stuck

in trees. A cat's claws curve inwards, so they can easily grip onto bark when they are travelling upwards, but they have difficulty descending the same way.

Indoor cats can still benefit from climbing if you provide a carpeted cat tree, which will give them a good workout, double up as a scratching post and make them less likely to destroy the furniture or scale the north face of the refrigerator. The more vertical areas your cat can access, the greater his territory, especially in a multi-cat household. So if you have lots of cats, providing climbing opportunities will reduce conflicts between them and give increased security to the more timid ones.

CHASING
Dots Of
LIGHT

CATS ARE NATURAL HUNTERS SO WHEN A LITTLE RED DOT DARTS AROUND THE FLOOR AND WALLS IT IS MOUTH-WATERING. WHO CAN RESIST A MOUSE THAT CAN WALK UP WALLS, EVEN FLY? YOUR CAT CAN'T, THAT'S FOR SURE. A BIRD-MOUSE IS THE ULTIMATE CHALLENGE.

The attraction of the laser pointer (or lazy pointer as it should correctly be termed, since cat owners can sit on the sofa while giving their cats a crazy workout) is obvious: it's small, bright, changes direction abruptly and moves at different speeds, just like prey. What's more interesting is that cats never seems to learn that they're chasing an apparition, a two-dimensional sprite they are doomed never to catch.

Suspend disbelief

Before you give yourself a hernia laughing at your cat's stupidity, consider that humans suspend their disbelief regularly when they seek entertainment and your cat can do this too. Gamers spend hours staring at television screens, shooting, running, jumping, collecting – fully immersed in the action and reacting to the triumphs and failures with real emotions. Furthermore, these screen images are made up of millions of tiny pixels – dots of light.

Capture

The burning question is whether your cat is psychologically damaged by chasing a mirage. Some cat experts believe it can be and suggest some strategies to provide the satisfaction of the capture. First, don't let the laser pointer be your cat's only toy. She needs a range, including wand toys that she can capture. Have some stuffed toys nearby (you could even stick some food inside them) and let the laser point come to rest on one of them during the hunt. Your cat can then take out her frustrations on the toy and you can switch off the pointer.

Hating DOGS

THE MUTUAL HATRED BETWEEN CATS AND DOGS IS A WELL-WORN TROPE THAT APPEARS REGULARLY IN POPULAR CULTURE. BUT WHAT'S THE REAL STORY WITH THESE TWO CARNIVORES?

Are they natural enemies or have we got it all wrong? Cats and dogs can be trained to live peacefully together under the same roof, but in the wild they can prey on each other. Lions will eat African wild dogs, wolves eat wildcats, coyotes will attack alley cats.

Domestic cats and dogs don't really hate each other, but the species think and act differently, so when they meet, their contrasting approaches to life are doomed to cause conflict. When a strange cat and dog meet, the cat will be naturally cautious but the dog's instinct is to bound over, full of curiosity and playfulness with his tail wagging broadly from side to side. The cat interprets the wagging tail and the bounding approach as threats and starts running; the dog misinterprets this as an invitation to play chase and friendship fails to blossom.

Socialize

If you want to create a mixed household, you have to start with the dog – bring them together with the dog on its leash. Reward him for staying calm and reward the cat for sticking around. If you can manage to rein in your dog's rambunctiousness around cats they can begin to form a mutual tolerance (reinforced with plenty of praise and treats all round from you). The best way to socialize them is during the sensitive bonding period (4–8 weeks for kittens, 5–12 weeks for puppies). If a kitten and puppy are raised together there is no reason why they can't grow into good pals in adulthood.